TABLE OF CONTENTS

Section	Subject Matter	Page
Foreword	Introduction and Copyright	1
I.	Background	3
II.	Overview	5
III.	Where To Begin	6
IV.	Your "Campaign" Materials	16
V.	The Interview	24
VI.	The Waiting	28
VII.	Polishing Your Interview Skills	30

Sample Materials

1. Letterhead Stationery
2. Letterhead Second Sheet
3. Letterhead Envelope
4. Introductory Letter
5. Resume Cover Letter
6. Resume
7. Telephone Script
8. Interview Checklist
9. Reference Sheet
10. Interview Questions and Answers
11. Thank You Letter
12. Paper for Taking Notes

FOREWORD

This proven "How to..." guide is just that! It contains easy-to-read and follow instructions, and explicit examples of materials you'll need to market yourself. After all, that's what you'll be doing: Selling others on what you've done and are capable of doing for them.

It takes thinking, hard work, patience, and time. We've helped by developing a system that has worked well for us and others. **It also will work for you!** But, you must follow faithfully the recommended procedures.

Unfortunately, there are few shortcuts to finding the right job or shifting careers. Or, just starting out after graduating from high school, college, or a technical school. Success in landing the right position in the end will depend upon you and your determination.

A well planned and executed job search can achieve an 85% to 90% success rate.

At some time in our lives, most of us will seek employment. As secretaries. Computer programmers. File clerks. Draftsmen. Welders. Student interns. Executives. Or, as other types of managers. Perhaps we have been dismissed, down-sized, or laid off, or our jobs eliminated through technological advances. It could be we're seeking our first job out of college or trade school.

Or, maybe the effects of a sluggish economy were too much for our businesses, or we were stymied in dead-end jobs and wanted to move into completely new or more exciting fields. Regardless, the negatives of being unemployed always are the same. We need work to pay for the steadily increasing costs of food, clothing, shelter, health care, and transportation.

> *Regardless of our reason for being unemployed, the key is finding work as quickly, easily, and cost-effectively as possible*

> *According to the most current Department Of Labor figures, nearly 6 million Americans are out of work - and competing for jobs in industries and businesses that continue down-sizing.*

> *To find work today, you have to be smarter, better, and recognized for what you "bring to the table."*

> *"Selling yourself" means clearly illustrating to a prospective employer the benefits you can bring to his or her organization.*

The problem is, at any one time there are hundreds of thousands - in fact millions - of other people in the same situation: Out of work, and looking and competing for job openings.

The ones who will win those positions will know how to effectively "sell" themselves and their abilities. They will know how to turn past accomplishments into promises of concrete benefits for the companies, organizations, or institutions hiring them. And, they will know how to set themselves above the majority of other job applicants when they go through the interview process.

Most people don't know how to do this; how to market their skills and talents. This book is dedicated to them, for it details the entire process simply and systematically. And, it requires only reading and following. You'll find note paper in Sample 12 at the back of the book, and as you read, you can jot down thoughts and "to do" lists. Above all, keep focused and positive. And, best of luck in your search!

Best of luck in your search!
– The Editors

Copyright © 1982 and 2001 by Employment Systems Associates, LLC. (a division of McCormick Associates, LLC). All rights reserved. ISBN: 978-0-615-26109-6

This document may not be down-loaded or copied in part or full without the expressed written permission from the publisher. All violations will be prosecuted to the fullest extent of the law. This copyright includes all text, recordings, graphics, trademarks, and logos, as well as sample documents, keywords, and description verbiage. Everything associated with our Web Site is protected under U.S. and international copyright law. Should legal action be warranted, all actions will be filed and heard in a Saint Louis, Missouri, court of law.

Any rights not expressly granted herein are reserved.

I. Background

First, let us state explicitly that we are not job search firms, management consultants, personnel officers, human resource managers, placement agencies, or "headhunters." We simply were faced with the task of finding work ourselves - which led to researching, comparing, critiquing, and "tweaking" the various job-hunting processes and procedures on the market.

The problem with most other approaches is they assume someone who is unemployed has several months during which he or she can complete self-examinations, take myriad skills assessments, plot Astro charts, and bio-rhythms. In the meantime, rent or mortgage payments come due; monthly payments for automobiles, utilities, and other essential items must be made; and, clothing and food requirements fulfilled. Not to mention, with loss of employment also comes loss of benefits: Health, life, and disability insurance.

> *Our time-tested, easy-to-use approach involves upfront planning and hard work. However, you can implement it in only a few weeks, with positive results possible within a month.*

> *As soon as possible after you become unemployed, stop by your closest Department Of Labor (DOL) office and sign up for benefits. You earned them...you deserve them...go ahead and collect them!*

> *In addition to income, you'll have access to valuable DOL information sources, including office equipment, work space, and services you can apply in your job search.*

With this in mind - especially if you are out of work - **one of your first priorities** should be finding an immediate source of income. If you've been employed up to this point, you probably have unemployment compensation coming from your state.

Admittedly, it's a difficult thing for people who have worked hard to request unemployment. "Go on the dole," as they say in Europe. It's like there's a stigma attached to being laid off, down-sized, or let go. However, while you were working you paid into a fund for this exact purpose, and now is the time to take advantage of those payments. Swallow your pride, visit your local Department Of Labor, and sign up. **It's your money, so use it to cover expenses while you're job hunting!**

Another reason for you to go to the Department Of Labor is to avail yourself of the services offered through its **Career Center**. At the Center, you'll get help with job hunting, veteran's groups, Job Corps Training, and vocational rehabilitation. And, if you don't have access to a computer, the Internet, copy and fax machines, and other office equipment, you'll find all these items there - as well as a resource room and myriad job listings. Again, **you've paid for these services, so take advantage of them!**

As mentioned earlier, when we suddenly were without work we did our homework and reviewed most of the job-hunting guides that were available. What evolved out of our research is the step-by-step system that follows. It has worked well for us in locating and changing jobs, and for hundreds of others who applied it. It was they who recognized a need for our proven approach, and suggested making it available in book form - as well as on the Internet - for others to use.

Ground work for this book entailed reading, studying, and condensing various pieces of literature written about job hunting, preparing resumes, interviewing, and developing associated materials. In essence, this guide is a compilation of the best thought and discussion concerning successful job hunting. And, it will work if strictly adhered to.

> *This updated version of our "Knock Three Times..." book is dedicated to those who have used the system successfully to find, improve, or change their careers.*

II. Overview

Our proven system works effectively for seasoned professionals, new graduates, and career-changers.

It's important for you to recognize that the end result of your job search should benefit two people: you, and the person hiring you. Everything contained in this guide is dedicated to bringing you two together. It shows you how to demonstrate to that person how he or she will benefit from hiring you. And, it illustrates how you must make yourself look and sound better than others out there competing for the same jobs. Realize, **upfront**, that you never get a second chance at making a strong first impression!

Whether you're a recent high school, trade school, or college graduate - beginning secretary, down-sized laborer, or seasoned executive - you've recorded positive accomplishments about which you may talk. We'll show you how, so the person doing the hiring knows what benefits you're bringing to the table.

At the rear of this guide are **samples of effective materials** and letters like those used in several successful job-getting campaigns. Adapt these to your own needs. They're yours to follow...and they work, believe us!

For an approximate idea of how much time is involved, you'll need at least two weeks to develop materials, and another two for mailing them. During this period of time, however, you'll be busy locating the right people to whom you'll write. Once you have materials and addressees, you're ready to seek your ultimate goal: Interviews.

> *Remember...you only get one chance at making a strong first impression. Make certain you reflect confidence and quality in your contacts with prospective employers.*

As far as costs are concerned, spend as little or as much as you wish. **Remember**, however, the materials you employ should reflect quality in the eyes of the recipients or prospective employers. Companies and organizations live by the adage, "You get what you pay for!" Quality is that important first impression we mentioned earlier.

One other thing to consider: When companies dismiss, right-size, or lay off employees, quite often guilt feelings come into play. In many instances, companies are willing to help ex-employees locate other work, and will bear the cost of job-hunting materials and services. It wouldn't hurt to approach your former employer about covering or sharing those costs.

III. WHERE TO BEGIN

Above all else, keep in mind that you are offering prospective employers an important and valuable commodity: Yourself! In the truest sense of the word, you are selling yourself and your talents. Therefore, you must market what you're offering in the most attractive, attention-getting, and effective manner possible.

With this goal in mind, our system then becomes a direct mail campaign that reaches the right person and convinces him or her to interview you as a job candidate, or consider you promising enough that a new position may be created. In many instances - as users of our system report - such has been the case. An organization or individual may not have a slot matching your particular skills, but may be impressed enough by your potential that he or she will develop a **new position**, or keep you at the top of the list for when the right opening does occur.

> *Several times our approach has resulted in employers creating jobs that didn't exist, based on the experience, skills, and benefits presented and promoted.*

Cardinal Rule 1: If at all possible, avoid blindly writing the prospective employer's Human Resources (HR) department. HR departments play valuable roles in interviewing, testing, hiring, training, and placing entry-level, clerical, and secretarial help. However, they rarely have "final hire" responsibilities for professional, supervisory, managerial, or executive positions outside their immediate department. Nor can HR effectively evaluate experience and accomplishments as realistically as can the person who knows he or she will have to live with the hiring decision.

> *Rather than writing to the Human Resources department, make a few calls and find the name, title, telephone number, and address of the person who actually has the hiring authority.*

Even though the HR specialist originally may not have chosen your application or resume for an interview, he or she will never override a direct request from an operations person to **specifically** interview you. Keep in mind, there are two different cultures within any organization - support and operations. If you are looking for a position in the support arena, Human Resources will play a significantly more important role in the selection process.

> *A critical first step is locating the right individual within the organization to whom you can direct your powerful communications.*

However, if you are looking for a position in the operations arena, HR will have little or no input into the selection process. Too, bear in mind that HR is not always informed of important openings that exist, soon may exist, or could be created **especially for you**.

For these reasons, it's crucial that you locate the right person to receive your correspondence. Even when answering "Help Wanted" ads - which result in interviews about five percent of the time - you can improve your odds dramatically. If the company's or organization's name is listed, call and identify the person responsible for your particular type of work and write directly to him or her.

This person with ultimate hiring authority will have an excellent opportunity to examine your background and get familiar with your capabilities first, even though, procedurally, he or she may be required to forward your letter to the Human Resources department. Therefore, make an effort in your letter to minimize alienating HR by sending that department's main contact person a courtesy copy of your letter.

Starting Your Job Search

Begin by determining what you're really after...a career or a job. Too much of our lives is spent at work to just settle for any job that comes along. By the same token, you may need work today; and can focus on career once income starts flowing in. Of course, the ideal situation if you're unhappy with your present job is to be employed and looking. As we said earlier, this book is dedicated to helping everyone find work.

> *Finding work is an all-consuming objective for someone who has lost a job and faces financial responsibilities. Worrying and blaming yourself won't help; whereas, a disciplined and sound job-hunt approach and positive outlook will..*

Cardinal Rule 2: Don't panic! Sure, that's easy to say with no money coming in! But, finding the right job takes time. And, it's worth waiting for; from financial and job satisfaction points of view. As Confucius said, "Choose a job you love, and you'll never work a day in your life!"

Try to establish definitive career objectives. Do you want a change of field? A different geographic location? Want to work with a large company? A small company? Want to do mental or manual labor? What kind? Where? For how much? Why?

Sit and list the things you expect from work, and the kinds of work you think would best fulfill those expectations. **Be honest with yourself.** If you truthfully can determine the kind of work you like and want to do, then it's simply a matter of locating where it is being offered. Following are a few good ways to begin looking:

> *A good place to start your job search is with friends, relatives, neighbors, or other acquaintances who may provide job leads or help you "network" with other key individuals*

A. Ask people you know if they've heard about jobs that are available (including family, friends, associates, peers, and neighbors): This probably represents your most reliable source of job leads (the **majority of work** is found in this manner), and typically these people will have specific contact persons in mind. If not, call and ferret out that individual's name (correct spelling, please), title, address, and secretary's name (for future calls - extra politeness in this instance will pay off).

Perhaps someone you know works for a company in which you're interested. If so, ask him or her for the name of the person to whom you should write. In addition, if your friend has influence within the company, inquire about using him or her as a reference, and mentioning his or her name in your cover letter.

If you connect, remember to thank this person with a letter of appreciation and a nice meal or small gift, either of which certainly is deserved for providing support and assistance.

> *Your local library has a reference room that can provide invaluable tools and information, and help you focus on your job search requirements.*

B. Visit The Library: The reference room in your local library is a good place to begin your own research. If you're not familiar with its contents, the librarian probably will be willing to suggest sources or help you locate publications that contain the names of people and companies to whom you should write. In addition, the reference room probably has other books on job-hunting from which you may glean a tip or two.

Following are typical publications worth mining:

1. *Standard & Poors:* These hefty volumes provide corporate descriptions, details on affiliate organizations, addresses, product or service information, and lists of key executives.

2. *Moody's (for the current year):* This handbook of common stocks offers company backgrounds, recent developments, business outlooks, names of officers, and addresses and telephone numbers of principal locations.

3. *Directory of Corporate Affiliations (for the current year):* This publication is the "family tree" of major corporations in America. It lists dollar volumes of sales, products, key executives, and numbers of employees.

4. *State Publications:* Most states publish directories of companies or firms involved in specific fields such as accounting, architecture, engineering, law, manufacturing, mining, and refining. Additionally, they publish listings of their 100 largest companies. These are valuable in locating the right people and companies according to industry and even geographic location.

5. *Professional Group Publications:* Most professional organizations produce their own publications - such as the roster of advertising and public relations shops that belong to the American Association of Advertising Agencies and Public Relations Society of America. There also are "sales rep" organizations that meet regularly within cities throughout the United States. You may pay a small membership fee to attend their functions, but it's worth it to network with those interested in the same things as you. And, of course, these contacts might know of job leads.

6. *The Yellow Pages:* Let your fingers look for companies and organizations listed under the heading for the field in which you're interested. Then, call to obtain the right person's name, telephone number, and information about the company.

While you're looking for that key contact within an organization, jot down pertinent facts about sales, products, services, earnings, or other areas where your strengths may be highlighted as benefits.

All major cities have their own "Business Journals" that feature articles about local companies and organizations. Typically, they publish rosters of these organizations that can provide excellent company and personnel data for job seekers.

If you respond to "Help Wanted" ads as another source of job leads, make certain you address job requirements in a manner that clearly helps the recipient recognize the benefits you can bring to the situation.

C. Read The "Help Wanted" Ads: As mentioned earlier, these pay back small returns for the numbers of people who respond with resumes. (It's been said that advertised jobs amount to **about one percent** of positions available in the U.S.) Another fact to keep in mind: Advertised jobs often are nothing more than an effort to meet federal or state obligations, and in reality the position actually is filled from within. (While it doesn't hurt to have more than one pole in the water, keep material and postage expenses in mind.)

Visit the major daily newspaper in your city and buy back issues of the edition that carries the most want ads (generally, it's the Sunday edition). Buy back issues for the past six to eight weeks.

Scan the ads under the heading for the type of work you seek. Don't be concerned should you find the ideal job listed in a notice that has been running for more than a month. Chances are, the HR department or individual who placed the ad still is sorting through resumes or applications.

Companies placing help wanted ads frequently allow up to three months to fill positions. Your chances of being recognized actually are better if your letter is the last to arrive on top of the stack!

Another piece of information for help wanted ads - don't worry about meeting all the criteria outlined. If the ad lists four or five requirements - and you only possess three - respond anyway, putting your qualifications forward as benefits you can bring to the job (discussed later under developing materials).

> *Don't be intimidated by cold calling. After all, it's your future. Plus, the contact you make may be aware of other companies that are looking. Develop a list of companies that offer the type of work you're seeking, telephone them, locate the individual who would have the hiring authority, and talk with him or her about how you could benefit the organization.*

> *A more subtle approach is calling and arranging an "information gathering" visit - which removes the stigma and stress of an interview (which, in a way, it is!). Ask to visit the department in which you're interested so you can learn firsthand what goes on in the "real world."*

D. Telephone Organizations: Carry **Number 6** above a little further, and while gathering information on the right contact person, inquire about work in your field of interest. It's not difficult to talk with strangers on the telephone when you simply realize they're somewhere else and of no threat to you. They may hang up, or behave rudely. But, what has that cost you? Only a few minutes of your time, and some minor discomfort. However, nine times out of ten you'll easily discover the full name, title, and correct address of the person to whom you should write.

> *Research the organization as well as the key contact. You may need this information later during the interview process.*

It's a good idea at this point to obtain as much information as possible about companies to which you'll be sending letters. Most provide **free** annual reports, sales brochures, or company publications (such as newsletters) to anyone requesting them. And, such materials will help you two ways: First, you'll learn quickly if you're really interested in the organization. Second, you'll be knowledgeable when it comes to fielding questions during the interview.

> *Employment agencies typically charge fees for helping people find jobs. And, recruiters and headhunters work for client companies; they are not your agents!*

Cardinal Rule 3: It's critical that you learn all you can about the companies in which you're interested. Prospective employers seldom will be interested in you if you don't show interest in them. Do a little homework...and be prepared! (Refer to the Checklist in **Sample 8**.)

In fact, develop a list of questions about the organization to which you'd appreciate answers. That topic will arise during the interview, and it's impressive to say, "Yes...I do have a few questions," and pull out your list. Immediately, the interviewer will recognize and note your preparedness.

E. Using Professional Agencies: Such firms include a litany of names, including headhunters, recruiters, executive search firms, employment agencies, and management consultants. By and large, headhunters, private employment agencies, and executive search firms can't help the bulk of job seekers - although they do account for as much as 40 percent of executive level placements.

> *Although women job-seekers are enjoying more success overall than men, our three-step system works effectively for either group.*

So, for those in upper income levels or technical or special fields (for example, computer science, Internet technologies, and aerospace), these organizations may be worth considering (in addition to all other search options). Remember, **search firms do not work for the person seeking work**. They work for employers, and typically have agreements with these clients to fill specific positions.

> *Conducting a job search on the Internet involves a "shotgun" versus "targeted" approach. However, we've included the top 12 Web Sites so you can expand your hunting territory!*

Never expect one of these firms to find a job specifically for you. Their fees are paid by client companies. Nor should you **sign or agree** to contract such services unless they are "**fee paid**," which means the organization seeking to fill a position will pay the firm or agency to find qualified candidates. As you consider the various means of finding work that are discussed in this book, consider interviewing with a headhunter as one of the **least likely** to result in your landing the job you want.

A good rule of thumb: If the headhunter contacts you first, you may end up in the 25 percent success category. If you contact the headhunter first, your placement odds are miniscule. Another rule of thumb: If you are unemployed, your chances of finding work through a headhunter are further diminished. Typically, these agencies work assignments with fairly long lead times.

A Word Of Note: Over the last 10 to 15 years - due to the disparity in salaries (the "Glass Ceiling" syndrome) - female job hunters have enjoyed more success in exercising this method than their male counterparts; possibly because certain "targeted" jobs require filling with women applicants.

> *Most especially on the Internet, your letters and resume must be attention-getting and powerful. The benefits you bring to the organization must be clearly stated and substantiated by past performance.*

F. Prospecting For Work On The Internet: Like responding to "Help Wanted" ads, finding work on the Internet by posting resumes to the myriad job-hunting search engines represents the "shotgun" approach.

However, there are methods you can employ on the Internet to help increase your job search results. As mentioned earlier, **finding a job** is the primary objective, and any means that will help us do so is worth considering.

Responding to job openings on the Net typically does not allow you to employ our three-step system. However, you always can use an effective cover letter to set the stage and highlight the "benefit" areas more fully outlined in your resume. Refer to the "follow-up" letter in the back of the guide (**Sample 5**) as a good starting point for developing your e-mail cover letter.

> *You may be interviewed via the telephone, and need to address such items as: Current employment status; brief background or experience; salary and relocation requirements; and, availability.*

> *Most Internet job search sites let you view jobs according to criteria you enter, and even respond with cover letters and resumes.*

> *While the odds of locating a job on the Internet today are pretty slim, it's yet another way of getting your resume before a reviewer who meets the criteria you select. Who knows, you may be lucky enough to "fill the bill" for an employer who opts to recruit employees in this manner.*

> *As more and more organizations turn to the Internet to recruit talent and survey the job market, more and more job search and employment firms will turn to this medium to find prospective job-seekers who meet their "client" criteria.*

Focus on one or two main benefits you have to offer - these should echo the criteria outlined in the prospective employer's "help wanted" ad - and explain how you can make his or her organization more successful.

Then, refer to the attached or pasted-in resume. **Regarding your resume:** Since your resume probably will be computer-scanned, make sure to select a typeface that scans well without some letters or numbers being confused with others. (Which is why we recommend **Times New Roman**.)

Per usual, thank the employer for considering your application, and volunteer to answer questions via e-mail, telephone, facsimile, or letter if he or she so desires. (Be sure you include these items.)

If you're qualified or lucky enough to attract the attention of an Internet recruiter, you may be interviewed (or "screened") via a telephone call. To prepare for this telephone conversation, refer to our questions and answers (**Sample 10**) for suggested responses to typical questions. Even better, order our "**Effective Interview Techniques**" CDs at http://stores.lulu.com/propman01

An Internet Tip: In the "Subject" heading box, don't enter "Resume of..." The search engine automatically will pick this up and file your resume with the myriad others that use the same subject. Better to use, "John/Jane J. Jobhunter Resume." At least this way your name is introduced and a first impression made!

Following are 15 of the top job search "engines." There are many others that specialize in academic, retail, writing or at-home jobs, or are listed on corporate web sites under "employment." Most of these engines enable you to create or paste a resume on their web sites:

► America's Employers (http://www.net-temps.com): Offers thousands of contract and direct jobs, as well as job search and recruiting centers.

- CareerOneStop (http://www.careeronestop.org): Supported by various government agencies, it caters to job seekers and employers.
- Career Builder Network (http://www.careerbuilder.com): Offers more than 1.3 million jobs. Lets you post resume, and offers career advice.
- KForce Job Postings (http://www.kforce.com): Web-based staffing firm provides job leads and host of helpful career services.
- Construction Work (http://www.ConstructionGigs.com): Bills itself as: "A no nonsense employment site for the construction industry. Site is for all construction-related occupations."
- Job-Hunt Organization (http://www.job-hunt.org): Information and links to many sources of job opportunities, including the less obvious ones.
- JobsOnLine (http://www.jobsonline.net): If a job is posted anywhere online, chances are it's in the JobsOnLine database.
- Jobosity (http://www.jobosity.com): A job blog keeps you current with employment trends, interview tips, and job openings.
- Job Sleuth (http://www.jobsleuth.com): E-mails you job leads based on criteria you enter in several categories.
- HotJobs.com (http://www.hotjobs.yahoo.com): Companies pay fees to post jobs or search resumes. Lots of career "channels."
- Online Career Center (http://www.occ.com): One of earliest to employ Internet for recruiting purposes, and affiliated with Monster.com (below).
- 4 Work (http://www.4work.com): Like Job Sleuth, post your qualifications and desired location and 4 Work will e-mail you leads.
- Six Figure Jobs (http://www.6figurejobs.com): Provides leads, a newsletter, and job descriptions for positions with salaries of $100,000 and more.
- The Monster Board (http://www.monster.com): Monster indeed! Typically, nearly 500,000 job listings.
- Web Monkey (http://www.webmonkey.com): Provides web-specific job-hunting tips not found elsewhere.

G. Develop A Timetable (for whatever approaches you elect to implement): As mentioned earlier, it will take two weeks of mailings before you call to arrange interviews. Recent college, trade school, or high school graduates - or those who are about to graduate - should begin compiling lists of companies and organizations to write at least three months in advance of the end of the school term or semester. This is because of increased competition from classmates going after the same jobs, and travel arrangements that must be made for attending interviews.

> It's essential you approach your job-hunting tasks in a disciplined manner. The key to developing and implementing an effective campaign is preparing a master schedule of required events, and then sticking to it and revising or updating it as needed. Prepare a daily list of those critical activities you need to accomplish, and then focus on carrying them out.

Once you've compiled a list of people and organizations involved in the career area in which you hold a strong interest, it's time to implement the campaign that will make them want to employ you. For future reference - and to stay on top of progress being made as you make your various written and verbal contacts - be sure to jot down dates, times, names, and subject matter contained in letters or conversations.

If you have several contacts outstanding, you need to know at which point each is in the three-step approach. This planning ahead helps you avoid being sabotaged by holidays or vacations just at the critical juncture at which you must call for an interview.

Keep in mind that most companies and organizations operate on a fiscal year rather than on a calendar year. Most will begin working on budgets for the coming year in late summer, and firm them by late fall. So, **September, October, and November** are outstanding months for job hunting.

> Keep close track of where each contact is within the three-step process. Your previous contact with this person promised you'd be contacting him or her again "in the near future."

By the same token, those companies probably will implement their approved budgets early in the new year, and begin filling positions during the first quarter. So, **January, February, and March** also are good months in which to seek employment.

During the in-between months, you'll run the risk of conflicting with spring or summer vacations, or the holiday seasons and yearend slow-downs.

> September, October, and November are ideal months for conducting your job hunt. Most major companies fill vacancies at the start of the new calendar year.

IV. Your "Campaign" Materials

Included in your campaign will be two mailings: An introduction and accomplishments letter, and a short follow-up letter that introduces a copy of your hard-hitting formal resume. The second mailing is followed soon after by your personal telephone call, seeking to arrange an interview.

Before addressing the actual campaign, let's briefly discuss the materials you'll be creating and using.

The first rule of advertising is to **get the reader's attention**. You will do this by exhibiting quality - in appearance **and** content - as you present yourself and the benefits you have to offer prospective employers. For this reason, it's worth the minimal expense of having your mailing materials professionally prepared (like the samples in the back of this guide).

This will require talking with a local printer, commercial artist or illustrator, or job printer (such as KwikKopy, InstyPrint, or Kinko's), all of which are listed in the *Yellow Pages*. Any of these sources can recommend and provide the elements you need for your mailing pieces, including graphic design (artwork), style of typeface, and colors and kinds of ink and paper.

A neat, clean appearance will catch the reader's attention and make him or her more receptive to what you want to say. Spending time, effort, and a little money on your campaign illustrates that you are confident in your accomplishments and offerings, and want to put your best foot forward. At the same time, it shows **your respect** for the recipient (just as correct spelling and grammar do).

Consider how you would feel, and which would impress you most: A personalized attractive letter, or one that has been photocopied (indicating it probably went to several other people)? Incidentally, if your goal is to work in sales, marketing, communications, public relations, or advertising, what better upfront way to exhibit your talents for informing, persuading, and selling!

For that important first impression, your direct mail materials must reflect top quality.

> *You can customize our proven three-step system and respond to job leads posted on the Internet. Of course, you'll lose the critical advantage of making three distinct impressions ("knocks"). However, you'll be employing the same top-quality materials and approaches we outline throughout this guide.*

> *Show respect for the recipient. Correct spelling, proper English, and to-the-point writing enables him or her to grasp your capabilities quickly and easily.*

> *Most direct mail experts agree it takes at least three "knocks" or impressions to penetrate a recipient's mind and cause him or her to pay attention to the message being sent.*

There are two major reasons why your direct mail campaign will work: First, it's been proven in advertising and direct mail selling that **you need more than a single "knock" or "impression"** to be effective. In fact, the ideal number of knocks is three (which is exactly what you'll do - make three distinctive impressions upon your prospective employer!).

Second, it's easier to organize and express thoughts and talents in writing. You'll be less likely to omit accomplishments, and you'll have the opportunities of polishing and refining your messages. Such is not possible with just a cold telephone call.

> *Your envelope represents the first impression the prospective employer will have of you. It needs to reflect professionalism and quality. For example, which would appeal more to you: A neatly addressed envelope, or one bearing a stick-on label?*

Additionally, letters have an enduring quality and carry more credibility. Plus, recipients may read them in private and at their own convenience (which is important for busy managers).

The number of letters you write obviously will determine the quantities of letterhead stationery, envelopes, resumes, and reference sheets you require. Plan for several extras of everything to allow for accidents or mistakes, or new names that inevitably will materialize later on.

The design of your materials should not be flamboyant, but should have a distinctive and professional look that will catch and hold the reader's attention and interest.

A. Typeset Versus Computer-Generated:

Professional looking materials (such as headings and artwork for the letterhead, second sheet, envelope, resume, and reference list included in the back of this guide) generally are set in type rather than being prepared on a computer. The quality is better, and it's more cost-effective. The letters you will write, of course, can be prepared on a computer.

> *Effective campaign materials can capture reader attention, create interest, and effectively communicate your abilities.*

Typesetting involves some expense, but the quality is well worth it. If you prefer to have materials typeset, select a typeface (or look) that appears to go hand-in-hand with the taste and personality you're trying to reflect.

Your printer, graphic designer, or artist will help you select a typeface. Once you've found one that suits, it may be strengthened or made less "aggressive" by setting it in a bold, medium, or light face. Whatever you do, don't mix typefaces! (Although, you may have your materials printed in one typeface, and prepare your letters using another.)

> *Make sure your materials reflect professionalism and good taste.*

Here are three pleasing typefaces, and a few thoughts about the appearances of each. We've reduced the size to 10 point for these examples - however, we recommend **no smaller than 12 point** for your materials.

Arial (10 point) — This is a crisp, attractive, and contemporary typeface. It's Gothic (without serifs, or feet, on its letters), and is a nice light face for headings. **Here it is in bold**.

Times New Roman (10 point) — This is an easy-to-read Roman (serif) face. For this reason, it's widely used for business communications. **Here it is in bold**.

Helvetica (10 point) — This typeface - also sans-serif (without feet) - appears larger than Arial although they're the same point size. Like Arial, it's a nice delicate face for headings to break up solid paragraphs of Times New Roman. **Here it is in bold**.

> *Select a typeface that's attractive and easy to read, and paper that reflects a professional quality and tone.*

B. Printing:

Have your materials - stationery, envelopes, resume, and reference page - professionally printed and on quality paper. Your artist, illustrator, local printer, or job shop can suggest paper and ink to use. (**Hammermill Bond** is a good, moderately priced paper that's carried by most printers across the nation.)

This book is printed on **Exact Offset** in 70-pound grey, using **Navy blue ink** (PMS 534). The samples are printed on 24-pound **Neenah Classic Linen** (Monterey Sand color), again using Navy blue ink (PMS 534).

Your printer or job shop also can provide business size (Number 10) envelopes made from the same kind of paper, as well as suggest a nice complementary or contrasting ink. Keep in mind that materials **must** carry through the appearance of quality.

Generally, the larger quantity of items you have printed (the run), the lower your per-item cost. Often, printing another 50 or so letterheads or second sheets costs only a few dollars more (as illustrated in the prices below). The biggest expense in printing is getting the presses set to roll.

> *In producing materials, the bulk of expenses are for upfront preparation. Therefore, larger quantities usually result in a lower "per item" cost.*

The materials you'll need are quoted below in various quantities and at prices close to what you would receive from a typical local print shop or InstyPrint, KwikKopy, or Kinko's outlet:

Estimated Printing Costs:

Item	50	100	200	300
Print stationery	$53.00	$55.00	$68.00	$72.00
Print envelopes	$55.00	$58.00	$74.00	$79.00
Print resume (2-page)	$87.00	$90.00	$116.00	$131.00
Print reference sheet	$55.00	$57.00	$71.00	$76.00

Start with the number of companies to which you'll be writing to estimate quantities and printing prices. Also keep in mind, some printers or job shops will only print quantities of 100 or more.

> *Most print shops have developed and typeset myriad communications materials, and will gladly help you design a specific look and "feel" to your materials.*

Don't cut your quantities so close to the bone there are no extras for computer or printing errors, accidents, or newly discovered companies to write. And, be sure to include "Thank You," reference, and follow-up letters in your estimates. A safe bet is to overprint by 10 percent. You always may use the extras for personal correspondence.

In preparing the first two letters - and subsequent "Thank You" or follow-up communications - if you haven't access to a computer or professional electronic typewriter (a Brother or IBM Selectric, for example), or can't type, consider the following methods of improving the appearance of your materials.

> *When estimating quantities, keep in mind you'll be mailing two letters (three counting your "thank you" after an interview), as well as a two-page resume, and reference sheet (if asked for by the interviewer).*

First, locate a professional typist to handle the chore for you. Bulletin boards around a local campus or high school, or small printers, are good sources. In most locations, students and secretaries perform evening and weekend typing duties inexpensively. Rates may vary from a few dollars an hour up to five, but a "pro" can crank out a lot of letters in an hour's time.

Also, keep in mind that companies like Kinko's rent various types of computers on an hourly basis, and can print out your letters and envelopes in a quality manner. Kinko's charges in the range of $12 per hour, but if you've prepared in advance, you can develop a lot of letters over that period. It's also handy that most such companies are open **24 hours daily, seven days a week**. And, don't forget the resources available at your local **Department Of Labor** office.

> *Today, nearly everyone has access to a computer. If you don't, ask someone who does to help out, or visit your Department of Labor office. There also are business centers where you can use one on an hourly basis (most charge about $12 an hour). The money and time you save by automating your material preparation process - in addition to being able to tailor your letters to specific key persons - is well worth the minimal added expense.*

C. Preparing Your Letters:

The introductory letter that is sent first (see **Sample 4** at the back of guide) performs three tasks:

- ▶ It gets the reader's attention
- ▶ It comfortably introduces you, your qualifications, and accomplishments less formally than in a resume
- ▶ It succinctly informs the reader about the benefits you could bring to the company, organization, or institution

In developing this letter, list qualifications you feel are "selling points" - attributes that more or less are inherent in activities you've performed. You can turn these into benefits. For example, you served in the military, attended a special workshop or conference, or worked as a summer camp counselor. You easily can turn these selling points into benefits - which only involves discussing your achievements from the **reader's viewpoint**.

> *Your introductory letter instantly tells the reader what benefits you bring to the job...and, in an interesting, effective, and informative manner.*

For example, if you were a noncommissioned or commissioned officer in the military, you possess leadership and management skills that any company would see as valuable to its operations.

Perhaps you were selected as a representative to Boys' or Girls' State, or were active in Scouting. Such accomplishments reflect character, honesty, ability, and the desire to achieve. Again, all are enviable and marketable traits - from the reader's viewpoint.

> *Take the time required to turn qualifications and experience into benefits the reader will recognize and appreciate.*

Even if you were a camp counselor, you have demonstrated ambition, organization, trustworthiness, and the ability to interface with and lead and teach others. Companies continually seek these qualities in employees.

The point is, you probably possess desirable traits that you take for granted, that could be exactly what prospective employers are seeking in job applicants. Turning those traits into benefits means simply showing the reader how those traits could make his or her organization more successful. Good gas mileage is a **selling point**. Saving five bucks at the gas pump is a **benefit**.

No matter how insignificant an accomplishment may appear, list it. It always can be eliminated in the final draft if your letter exceeds two pages. It's often difficult - if not impossible - to judge what will touch the recipient's hot buttons.

To repeat: Selling points are qualifications you possess; benefits are those qualifications described in such a manner that the person to whom you're writing will quickly and easily recognize how those qualifications will help his or her organization, and match perfectly with its needs.

> *Your second letter highlights your key benefits, and serves to introduce your resume.*

When you list your accomplishments, relate them to what you have done for others. This way, it's easier for the recipient of your letter to transform in his or her own mind how you will benefit the organization. In other words, if you sold 20 cars a month for Smith's Auto Company, your recipient will figure you probably will do at least that good for him or her.

In fact, if he or she believes in the quality of his or her product or service - and the accomplishments you've listed - then he or she probably believes you could do **even better** in his or her employ, and could hire you on that basis alone!

The second letter you develop and mail (**Sample 5** at the back of the book) briefly reiterates your strongest qualifications. Keep this letter short and to the point. Its primary purpose is to introduce your formal resume (**Sample 6**), which then fills any gaps.

From information you've compiled on the company - along with materials you've read - extract what you consider the most pertinent point to address. If you recently read that the company is expanding its management training staff and facilities - and you're a veteran looking for this type of work - explain how your military background qualifies you in preparing, implementing, critiquing, improving, and supervising company training functions.

> *When listing your skills, accomplishments, and experiences, put yourself in the reader's shoes...ask yourself what would be most meaningful to you on the other side of the desk.*

This second letter also contains an "urge to action" - it closes by stating you'll call in the near future (a week) to arrange an interview at the recipient's convenience. **Often**, you will have heard from him or her by that time!

Again, the letters you send **must list** your most important qualifications and accomplishments couched in terms that show the reader how they will benefit him or her and the target company. Put yourself in his or her shoes. What would you be looking for in an employee if you were on the other side of the desk? Don't just list the things **you** want to say. Write the things **he or she** wants to hear!

> *For help developing your resume - and to ensure it's a powerful portrait of your performance - refer to Sample 6 at the back of this book.*

Your resume must address the qualifications you possess in a manner that will show the recipient what you have done, and can do for him or her. Keep extraneous "personal" information to a bare minimum, if you must mention it at all. Most professional resume developers and consultants advise against including personal information, because you never know what will alienate the person reading it.

> *In developing your resume, it's safest to avoid including "personal" attributes: For example, health, marital status, kids, hobbies, and favorite sports. You never know what the reader may find objectionable.*

For example, if you list a spouse and three children - and the reader is unable to have children or is divorced - that item might be held against you. The same holds true with height and weight, which might disturb a reader who is short, heavy, or physique-conscious.

It often has been said that a resume can hurt, as much as it can help. Sometimes, reviewers go through resumes with the intent of casting out as many as possible, and narrowing the field of search. If such is the case, they most certainly would focus on personal aspects which really don't strengthen the benefits you bring to the job.

In summary, your timetable is as follows:

Week 1 - Send two-page introduction and accomplishments letter. Mail on Thursday or Friday to arrive Tuesday or Wednesday. The bulk of most business mail arrives on Mondays, so you don't want to get lost in the shuffle. By the same token, mail arriving on Friday often is put on hold until after the weekend. We also advise you use a **commemorative stamp** to dress up your envelope and make your letters stand out from the rest. Whatever you do, avoid using your current employer's postage meter!

> *The entire job search system effectively can be implemented in a month's time!*

Week 2 - Wait a full week after mailing the first letter, and send the second one with a resume enclosed. In this letter, you're telling the person you're writing that you'll soon be calling. Chances are, you may not have to!

> *When you call to arrange an interview, be confident, friendly, and courteous.*

Week 3 - Wait another seven days. If you haven't heard from the prospective employer, call to arrange your interview. By then, unless he or she has been out of town or terribly busy, the recipient knows about you and could want to see you. Frequently, you'll be congratulated for developing and implementing an effective direct mail program - even when openings do not exist. In several instances, users of our approach have reported their target companies "created" jobs that did not exist based on qualifications and benefits they outlined in their letters and resume.

> *The script should enable you to set a date, time, and place for a meeting at the contact's convenience.*

See the suggested script (**Sample 7**) at the back of this book for help with your telephone call. Don't read the script over the telephone! Memorize it, rehearse it, get comfortable with it, then practice introducing yourself to friends on the telephone to ensure you don't come across like a recorded announcement.

Granted, there occasionally are obstacles to your getting through to your targeted contact. One of these is the secretary who acts like a Marine master gunnery sergeant and won't let you past regardless of how pleasant you may be. Sometimes, you can get around this protective barrier by calling earlier in the morning or later in the evening, and reaching the boss directly.

V. The Interview

In preparing for interviews, complete the Checklist you'll find as **Sample 8**. It will be invaluable in helping you get ready and stay on track. Above all, be on time for the interview...or a few minutes early. It's a good idea to make a trial run to the location if you've never been there before. Remember, **Murphy's Law!**

Make sure you're dressed appropriately. Generally, coat and tie for men; dress, suit, or skirt and jacket for women. Granted, a lot of organizations now dress "business casual" in slacks and golf shirts. However, unless the person you're going to interview says to show up in this attire, stick with the more traditional dress code.

> *Never arrive late for an interview. In fact, going on a practice run before-hand to gauge traffic and parking challenges is an excellent idea.*

Be pleasant, and look the interviewer directly in the eye (it's easier to concentrate on just one!). Try to relax and enjoy yourself, and remain focused on why you're there and the points you want to get across. Interviews often are tense and stressful situations - for you **and** the interviewer. And, it's worse than a typical meeting of strangers, because you're both trying to communicate and, at the same time, get to know the other individual.

> *Be prepared: Know the organization, and have meaningful questions prepared and ready to use when called upon.*

Wear a relaxed smile, act friendly, and be "humble": In other words, you're there to listen, learn, and provide information. Don't be a "know it all." Most often, your interviewer will pick up on your positive attitude and return the favor. Above all, be motivated and enthusiastic. Again, one of the traits the interviewer will assess is your body language (the important other half of the interview equation).

Be honest in your answers. The last thing you need is to trip over some exaggeration or claim that comes home to roost later in the interview. Stand on your own experience and the value you know you can bring to the organization.

> *You can be truthful in your responses, and still put a positive spin on your answers. If you've just recently graduated from college, there's nothing wrong with admitting you'll be in a "learning curve" until you gain experience on the job. Even so, you probably can come up with examples of how you're a "quick study" on new projects.*

If you're a recent graduate - and searching for that important first job - don't be afraid to admit you'll need help as you work to gain "hands-on" experience in the working world beyond the campus. Most interviewers will recognize this upfront, and probably can visualize how your accomplishments in school will become benefits to the organization as you mature in your job.

Some companies even prefer new hires right out of college, and recruit on campus or at "Job Fairs." (Be sure to touch base with your placement or guidance counselor to uncover these opportunities.) Also, keep in mind that some colleges and universities are interested in helping alumni - most with more than just an eye toward annual solicitations and contributions - and maintain up-to-date lists of U.S. employers and jobs available. Regardless of when you graduated, contact your alma mater and inquire about such services. And, yes, it would be nice (and appreciated) if you sent along a contribution or joined the alumni association! However, do not expect your alma mater to provide much more than search assistance, if that.

> *Another important source of job leads could be your college, university, high school, or trade school.*

> *Often, a second interview will be required. If this occurs, consider it another opportunity to "show your stuff." Replay the first session in your mind, jot down some notes, and think about how you can improve your performance during the next meeting.*

Interview Strategies:

One way to overcome much of the interview stress is to be fully prepared. Find out as much about the company or organization as possible, and how the position you're going after fits into its business plan. Now is when you would employ the Checklist in **Sample 8** and that list of questions you developed to ask the interviewer when called upon to do so.

Research the company's operations, products, sales, and current items of interest that may have appeared in recent newspaper articles. Know the organization's chief executives, and the kind of business year just concluded (most of which is included in company annual reports). What are its key markets, and areas where it intends to compete in the future? If it's not a global operation, is that planned in the short- or long-term? Who owns the organization, and what is the interviewer's tenure there?

> *During the interview, maintain eye contact and answer questions clearly and to the point. Don't ramble on after you've answered the question.*

During interviews, a number of general questions always crop up (see **Sample 10** at the back of the book). We've provided sound answers for a few difficult questions. More are available on our CDs, "**Effective Interview Techniques**," which you can purchase at http://stores.lulu.com/propman01

> *We offer inexpensive yet effective instructional CDs that can help you address the most stressful interview questions. Additionally, CDs provide insights into what the typical interviewer expects from the interviewee.*

Our presentation also offer tips from the **interviewer's point of view**.

If the interviewer asks for references, provide him or her with your prepared reference sheet (**Sample 9**). Make certain beforehand that everyone included on your list is aware that he or she is on it. In most instances, references seldom are called. However, be safe and thoughtful in advance, and ensure that telephone numbers and addresses are up to date.

> *You can order our "Effective Interview Techniques" CDs at http://stores.lulu.com/propman01*

It's seldom a good idea to volunteer references. If asked, you may provide them. But remember, you're bringing other opinions into the interview and hiring situation by doing so. And, sometimes, even the best reference or friend may say or mention something that can dampen your chances.

Let the interviewer do most of the questioning, and keep your answers short, simple, and to the point. Don't ramble on, or wander about! He or she is paid to determine the most qualified candidate and, therefore, should carry the bulk of the interview. While you don't want to purposefully avoid any issues that are brought up, don't necessarily volunteer any, either.

> *There are certain questions employers are not allowed to ask. You should be familiar with these prior to going on interviews, which could keep you from getting caught off-guard regarding personal subjects.*

Keep in mind that **under law**, there are some questions the interviewer cannot ask, such as age, marital status, religion, nationality, or financial condition. (We also cover these on our **Effective Interview Techniques** audio presentation.) However, there's no guarantee such questions won't come up. For this reason, confirm in your own mind how such a question relates to the job for which you are interviewing, and weigh what harm you would do to your effort by answering a question of dubious legal status. By not answering, you may give the impression that if employed you would become a "lawsuit in waiting."

As a precaution - before going on interviews - you might touch base with your state's Fair Employment Practices Commission to see if a list of such questions exists. You then could become familiar with it, and practice how you would respond...just in case.

During the interview, put a positive sheen on the answers you give. Above all, **never talk negatively** about previous employers, bosses, or situations in which you were involved. To toss in a few old cliches, what goes around comes around, and burning bridges can come back to haunt you should you ever have to cross them again!

Cardinal Rule 4: Finally, and **most important**, promptly send the interviewer a letter or note thanking him or her for the opportunities of meeting and talking about the company and its operations (see **Sample 11** at the back of the book). This letter also is an excellent vehicle for reiterating any pertinent points that arose during the interview, and further could relate what you have to offer.

It's also nice to send a short note of thanks to secretaries or others who helped while you were preparing or waiting for an interview.

And, certainly, send letters to any other staff members who were invited to participate in meeting with you on behalf of the company.

> *Be sure to send "thank you" letters to all who played a part in your interview.*

You need to take the time to "personalize" each letter: Refer to the primary comment or issue each participant raised, and address it in this "one-on-one" fashion. It will make an impressive impact, and you'll have one more person in your corner!

Frequently, performing such a simple act of common courtesy can spell the difference between receiving a job offer or rejection. We've heard of several cases where it was the deciding factor. Again, however, sending a "thank you" is a further reflection of the quality image you carried throughout your job-hunting process.

VI. THE WAITING

nce you've interviewed with a company, little more may be done other than being patient. The ball now is in the organization's court, and it's difficult to successfully speed the decision-making process without appearing overly anxious. At the conclusion of the interview, however, you have every right to ask when the hiring decision will be made.

In today's economy - with a tremendous number of people applying for every sort of job - a company may require several weeks just to sort through resumes, interview, and then reach a hiring decision. Time may be crucial to you - especially if you're currently unemployed - but companies will take all they feel is necessary to locate the best individuals for the jobs.

To help you with the waiting game, keep in mind this little poem sent to us by a dear friend while we awaited calls from prospective employers:

> Put up in a place,
> Where it's easy to see,
> This cryptic admonishment,
> T.T.T.
>
> When you think how depressingly
> Slowly you climb,
> It's good to remember,
> That "Things Take Time."

After you've received a firm offer, however, you have leverage in applying pressure on companies from which you've not received offers. Call the individual with whom you've interviewed, and inform him or her that you've been made an offer, and are obligated to respond by a certain date. Most often, this approach works!

> *While you're awaiting the results of your interview, rethink how you could have handled your campaign more effectively. "Lessons Learned" may help you do an even better job the next time out!*

> *Like anything else, the more practice you have at writing letters and handling interviews, the more skilled you'll be at selling yourself and your abilities.*

> *If you receive a job offer, you may use this to apply pressure to other interviewes who clearly were inerested but have not contacted you yet.*

It's a heady feeling to be in control of the situation at this point! However, **never** accept an offer immediately - take some time (a day or two) to think it over, and let the interviewer know when you will reach your decision. On the other hand, if you decide not to accept the offer, be sure to advise the interviewer of your reasons for not doing so as soon as possible.

That's all there is to selling yourself. Granted, this has been quite a lot to absorb. However, if you follow this book to the letter, the results will be well worth the efforts.

Good luck...and good selling!

It's difficult advice to follow if you've been out of work for a while, but never accept an offer immediately. Prospective employers will understand if you ask for time to consider the proposition. However, be sure to give the interviewer a specific time when you'll arrive at your decision.

VII. POLISHING YOUR INTERVIEW SKILLS

Part A - Top 20 Questions With Solid Answers: Following is a transcription of our "**Effective Interview Techniques**" presentation to assist you in preparing, organizing, and rehearsing for interviews. The answers and advice provided reflect current "best practices" in interview tips and tactics, formulated by job search experts. Now then, **you must tailor** and practice your answers so they reflect **your** skills, interests, and accomplishments. **Good luck!**

1. Do you work better alone, or as part of a team?

You need to talk about how you can get along with a variety of people. **Response:**

*"As you'll note on my resume, I have a strong track record of individual accomplishments where I was given deadlines and left to develop effective approaches. Even in such instances, however, I was still interacting as part of a team. I sought the most qualified sources of information, inside and outside of the company, and employed other resources as required. Other times, I helped achieve outstanding accomplishments as a member of a large team effort. I would say that - although I perform well independently - I am **always** part of the company team."*

2. What do you like most about your current job?

You need to demonstrate to the interviewer how you can help the company in the job for which you're applying. **Response:**

"Mainly, that I make a valuable contribution to my organization's profitability through my work efforts. I rely on 'feedback,' and if I see positive results, I'm encouraged. On the other hand, if I see a slump, I work hard to turn it around as quickly as possible."

3. Why do you want to leave your present job?

The interviewer will be concerned if you start raising issues or talking negatively about your current employer. Instead, put a **positive spin** on your answer by talking "career improvement." **Response:**

"My current employer is a comparatively small company in its field, and is being purchased by The Giant Corporation - which will use its own sales, marketing, and customer service departments. I could continue my career with Giant, and enhance my growth potential with the new organization. However, I've been researching your company and, after talking with you, am convinced this is the best opportunity at this point in my career."

4. What are your short- and long-range goals?

The interviewer is trying to see where you will fit into his or her organization in the near future, as well as down the road. Your response must indicate you've given serious thought to where you want to go, and how you'll get there. **Response:**

"Short term, I'll need to come up to speed in my new position, learning about my duties and how they relate to your company's future growth plans. Other priorities include becoming familiar with your corporate structure and culture, and developing the best methods for getting the most from each individual in my department. On a long-term basis, say 5 to 10 years, I plan to continue honing my skills and look forward to accepting your company's challenges to further my professional growth."

5. What can you tell me about yourself?

What the interviewer wants to hear clearly and succinctly is a quick recap of your education, skills, talents, and experience. **Response:**

"I graduated from City Community College with an Associates of Arts Degree in Business Administration, and went on to State University to get a Bachelor's in Accounting. I started my career as a staff accountant at The Small Firm, and have received several promotions - which have challenged me to continue building my skills and abilities. I've always received bonuses that reflect my contributions and value to the company and, in return, have always given 100% on the job. I've been a loyal employee, and maintain an uncompromising work ethic."

6. What do you feel is your greatest accomplishment?

In such an instance, focus on **your most recent** accomplishment and ensure it relates directly to the job for which you're interviewing. **Response:**

"One of my more impressive successes was early in my career at The Small Company, where I was responsible for improving public opinion after a freak accident had injured two workers. The local media made a circus of the whole affair, and our stock took a dive. I arranged a two-hour national press conference at our facility, including a full tour and presentation of our safety protocols. Less than one week after the incident, several national news programs and print media revealed to the public how our safety procedures actually exceeded Government standards, and thereby restored consumer confidence."

7. What do you like least about your current job?

Normally, you **should not** say anything negative about your past jobs, companies, or bosses. However, here's one way it may be skillfully done. **Response:**

"One thing is, my current employer's in-house staff is so much smaller than yours. They only staff their telephones from 9 a.m. until 5 p.m. Eastern time. Because of this, I frequently get complaints that this makes it difficult for reporters working on an evening deadline to reach us for basic information. Due to the upcoming buyout by Giant

Company, management chose not to change our telephone hours. For this reason, the 24-hour telephone coverage you have at Great Job not only appeals to me, but I consider much more professional."

---

8. Have you ever been fired?

Realistically, you've either been promoted out of, fired from, or quit any job you've ever left. If you were laid off or fired, it's best to address these concerns immediately. With the layoffs and downsizings occurring today, there's less stigma about being let go. Whatever you do, **don't focus on the negatives**. Talk about what you've learned from the experience. You can even turn termination into a positive!

Response:

"Actually, I had one job where my supervisor and I mutually decided I should leave. The first two years I worked for Gone Under & Associates, they were thriving. In the third year, new management continually questioned and reversed my decisions. After six months, we decided I was not effective in the position, and I left to accept my current position. One year after I left, Gone Under filed for bankruptcy."

---

9. What do you consider your strengths?

The interviewer in this line of questioning is trying to fit your skills, experience, and learning into his or her organization - ideally, within the position that needs to be filled. He or she needs to hear about the things you do well - and in a manner that translates easily into the benefits the organization will derive from hiring you. If you've done your homework - and know about the position for which you're applying - you can tailor your strengths specifically to that job.

Response:

"Let me tell you why I'm interviewing with your company. Your company is successful because it makes certain that quality and timeliness are paramount in fulfilling delivery of machinery orders. As manager of production for my current job, I developed a computerized checklist that ensured all parts were included, shipping instructions were

clear, and delivery schedules were met on time. My checklist saved the company nearly $1 million in shipping costs, and reduced customer complaints over missing parts by more than half during its first year of implementation."

10. Why are you applying for this position?

The interviewer wants to know what it is that turns you on to the job primarily, and company, secondarily. Here's your opportunity to demonstrate you've done your homework on the organization.
Response:

"I prefer to make informed decisions. I've done a fair amount of research into various companies. Great Job has the blend of qualities I feel suit my abilities to enhance sales and marketing efforts: solid products, a growing national market share, and plenty of room for further consumer awareness through sales promotion activities. Additionally, your stock performance and reports of quality working conditions and satisfactory compensation give me even more reasons to seek this position and align my goals with yours."

11. What would your current supervisor say about your job performance?

What the interviewer is hoping for is a recap of your last appraisal. If you provide one, ensure it corresponds with the real thing. Remember, your new employer may check on your references. The ideal situation is if you have a copy of the appraisal, and can discuss it with the interviewer. **Response:**

"My supervisor has written a number of congratulatory letters to me personally, and to my department as a whole. She also has recommended me for raises and extra performance-based bonuses. If questioned, I'm certain she would say I have excelled in every area of responsibility. In fact, I have a few of these letters with me if you would like to review them."

12. What was the worst mistake you ever made?

We all make mistakes. That's what the interviewer wants to hear. However, more important than that, he or she wants to be convinced you've learned from that mistake, and have put safeguards in place to ensure it never happens again. Like other work-related activities, positives can arise out of negatives. **Response:**

"There was a time we needed 5,000 widgets, and I signed a requisition prepared by a subordinate for 50,000 widgets at $1.25 each! The error was not noticed until the widgets hit our receiving department. Then, to complicate matters, the widget company was going out of business, so all sales were final! After negotiating a quantity discount - at a price of $1 per widget - I found a way to incorporate the widgets into a new marketing program. That netted us more than $100,000 in first time business over a four-month period. A conservative estimate revealed that we also received more than $150,000 profits directly related to the marketing campaign. Of course, since then I have been doubly careful about reviewing all documents before signing."

13. What is your biggest weakness

Much like the previous question, you're obligated to come up with something! Mistakes are part of the natural learning process. Typically, interviewers will focus on what you describe as a weakness, and see if it can be linked to other areas of exploration. Again, look for ways to put a **positive sheen** on what you describe as a weakness. **Response:**

"I'd say, over-planning. I have a strong natural tendency to conceive bizarre scenarios and make sure we have contingency plans for them. This can waste time. However, I prefer 'fire prevention' to putting out brush fires, anytime. I recently worked out formulas to help me determine whether certain circumstances are even remotely likely. In this manner, I can plan for everything that might really happen without wasting time on highly improbable events."

Other examples you might use in answering this question are:
"I tend to expect other employees to live up to my high standards."
"I take on too much myself to ensure the work gets done on time, within budget, and per specifications."
"I become impatient with delays, and must spend valuable time searching for ways to prevent bottlenecks."

14. How do you keep on top in the industry?

The interviewer expects you to be familiar with the various industry publications that discuss the most recent trends, practices, and procedures. **Response:**

"For industry-wide news, I read several print and on-line publications. I also scan the local newspapers to keep up with community events. Additionally, I spend one to two lunch breaks a week talking to people in my department and other areas to get an inside feel for what's happening in the company. I often learn more through these 'walk-arounds' than I do by reading about the other departments and divisions."

15. How are you at motivating people to work?

The interviewer is especially interested in learning that you recognize different people are motivated by different factors. Abraham Maslow in his "hierarchy of needs" defines five levels at which people are motivated by different desires. Incentive motivation agencies typically focus on Level IV, "Self-Esteem," as key to stimulating salespersons to increase their performances. **Response:**

"In my current position, as Paint Sales Supervisor, I recognize that each of the sales clerks who work in my department need encouragement in different ways. For some, just a simple 'nice job!' will do. Others are embarrassed if I make too big a deal out of a major sale. Still others are hurt if I don't notice every positive aspect of their day-to-day performances. I guess the learning point is: As long as you treat them fairly, respect them as employees, and let them know when they do great work, then you're performing as a supervisor should."

16. Do you mind traveling in your job?

Obviously, if you've done your homework, you know the job requires a certain amount of travel. If it is more than you anticipated - or as outlined in the job description - then raise the issue with the interviewer at this time. But, do so discreetly - especially if it will impact serious issues such as family responsibilities, health, or continuing education. **Response:**

"I understand the position requires a certain amount of time on the road, and I'm prepared to travel as needed. I'd like to point out, I'm currently enrolled in night classes at State University, and so would appreciate learning in advance if travel requirements are going to increase so I can revise class schedules and course requirements and ensure they don't interfere with performing my duties."

17. What are your salary requirements?

It's a good idea not to commit yourself. The ball is in the organization's court as far as making an offer is concerned, and what you're currently earning has nothing to do with that. If the subject keeps coming up, suggest a broad range - from $20,000 to $30,000, for example. Keep this in mind, also: Discussing salary is something that should occur **after** you've gotten through the important aspects of the job - including the work itself, who you'll be working for, who'll be working for you, and where your job fits into the overall operations of the organization. Discussing salary early only serves one purpose: to screen you out as too cheap or too expensive. For this reason, you need to politely delay such a discussion. Here's one approach. **Response:**

"I'm sure Great Job wants to pay me a fair salary based on my value to the company, so I'd rather spend time making sure that I'm the right person for the job before we discuss any offer."

Here's another approach to answering this question:
*"Salary is important, but so are the details such as the work I'll be doing, whom I'll be working with and for, and where my job fits into the organization. Do **you** have a particular salary range in mind?"*

18. When can you begin working for us?

If you've been fired, downsized, or laid off, of course you can begin immediately. However, if you're still employed, you must give a minimum of two weeks' notice - or more, if you're employed in a critical position, or one that must be advertised and then filled by a selection committee. Regardless of how interminable your current situation is, **don't burn bridges!** Treat everyone as you want to be treated. **Response:**

"I appreciate the job offer! I'll submit my resignation to my current employer tomorrow. I should be able to begin work in two weeks. However, I also would be happy to take home reading or study materials, and drop by on evenings or weekends to meet with staff, or other team members with whom I'll work."

It's wise **never** to accept a job immediately. Ask for a day or two to think it over. The interviewer will understand.

19. Are you willing to relocate?

It's extremely important that you're prepared and ready to ask questions when you go on your interviews. You must make certain that they're the right questions, and phrased appropriately. Take this question, for example. If relocation is a hot topic for you, be sure to ask about it at the right time, and in the right way. For example, if you blurt out, "Will I have to relocate!", the interviewer immediately will sense that you don't want to move. Here's a better way to handle this question when it comes up. **Response:**

"I realize it's often important to relocate for the company to use my skills and abilities to the fullest, and I'm fully prepared to move as necessary. How frequently could I expect to be relocated, say within a 10-year period?"

20. Illegal questions.

Every state has specific laws regarding what questions may or may not be asked during the interview situation. Questions regarding race, age, sex, religion, nationality, ethnic origin, health, finances, military service, sexual preference, criminal and police records, organizations to which you belong, and marital status are off limits. If you're subjected to such questions during an interview, you can file a formal complaint with the Equal Employment Opportunity Commission. **A good rule of thumb** is: If the question does not relate to the job for which you are interviewing - or the job you currently hold - then you can politely request not to respond. Just in case, here's a solid response to the question, "How does your husband/wife feel about your career?" **Response:**

"If I'm hearing you right, it seems like you're asking me a broad question. Let me assure you, there is nothing in my personal life that would prevent me from dedicating a full 100% to my career at Great Jobs."

Part B - What The Interviewer Expects:
The following transcript is from our "**Effective Interview Techniques**" presentation, and offers insightful observations by a Director of Human Resources for a major international company. Her outlook from "the other side of the desk" will help you plan and prepare for your interviews.

What challenges face candidates as they prepare to interview?

Often, the biggest challenge is the ability to sell yourself. You must demonstrate on personal and professional levels why you're the best person for the job.

> **What are the typical things that job applicants do wrong?**

Those candidates who do not invest the necessary time to prepare for the interview are most likely to present themselves poorly. It really shows when you ask them what special skills they bring to the job, or why they're interested in the position.

> **Conversely, what separates them from the successful candidates who present themselves properly?**

Candidates who are confident, prepared, and relaxed tend to be the most successful. Again, it's taking the time before the interview that really makes the difference. Make certain you know everything you can about the job, the organization, and your part in it.

> **Is there any other information or background that you'd like to share with us before we dive into the secrets of successfully undergoing the interview situation?**

An interview really is a two-way conversation. It's a chance for the candidate to tell the potential employer why he or she is the best person for the job - and, to find out if the organization is a good fit for him or her. Regardless of whether it's your first interview or your 100th, approach it positively, enthusiastically, and confidently.

> **You've broken down the interview process into three broad categories: before the interview, during the interview, and after the interview. What's your thinking?**

For me, the key word is "**process**." It's easy to get overwhelmed by everything that goes into preparing for, and undergoing, an interview. I believe by breaking the process down into steps, it's easier to organize, and manage, and not let yourself become overwhelmed. Of course, the quality you exhibit as you proceed through the various phases often depends on the upfront work you do researching the organization.

> **What is the preparatory stage before the interview? I notice you've broken it into three phases, too.**

One of the most important things a candidate can do is research the company, institution, or organization. Take the time to find out what the primary service or product is, check out financial stability, and know the **culture**. This helps you determine if this is a place where you want to work. Secondly, **know yourself**. Remember, the product you're selling is you, and every good sales person knows the product inside and out. And, third, dress the part. **First impressions are everything**. A study by UCLA a few years ago revealed that 55% of communication is non-verbal. That means a significant part of your performance during the interview is not going to be based on how you respond to the questions.

> **What do you mean by "culture" of the company?**

The culture of a company is based on the structure, values, behavior, and social norms that are supported by the organization. Every organization has its own internal culture, and you need to penetrate that.

> **Why is researching a company so important?**

Researching the organization is necessary to ensure the prospective job is a good fit for you. Also, you need to know specifically who has the hiring authority in the department or area in which you're interested. This is the person who will receive your personalized and targeted communications. Additionally, you'll need this kind of information for your subsequent interview. Remember, the interviewer **will expect you** to have questions. The internet also offers a wealth of company information and industry statistics. You can locate most major organizations there, and you can check their web sites for other job openings of interest. When researching a company, organization, or institution, pay attention to what you learn about its culture. Questions you can ask to help determine the culture are: Is it family friendly? Is it social as well as professional? What is the work/life balance? What is the employee balance - especially regarding male/female, minorities, and marrieds and singles? Know what you're looking for **before** the interview - this is the critical part of the research.

> *How can you get answers to such questions during the research stage?*

There are several ways. For example, reviewing an annual report will tell you how many officers of the company are males, females, and minorities. This will give you a clue about whether or not diversity is valued in the organization. Second, many organizations are recognized for their employee programs or civic sponsorships. For example, each year *Fortune* magazine lists the "Top 100" companies for which to work. You can check to see if the organization with which you're interviewing is listed there.

> *What questions can you ask during the interview to help determine the culture?*

A good one is, "How are employees recognized?" This will give you a feel for the type of recognition programs, and how the organization really feels about its employees. You also can ask, "How often are company meetings held?" - which offers insight into the importance of employee communications. You might also ask, "In what kind of partnerships or employee activities does your company participate?"

What's next after determining the prospective employer could be a good fit?

It's obviously important to understand the organization's products and services. Know its competitors, what its reputation is, and if there have been any recent major organizational changes. This gives you an idea of stability. You want to be with a company that's going to be there for the long haul. Any more, that's really important - and another reason to know the financial status of the organization. If it's publicly traded, know the ticker symbol and stock price. And, as mentioned earlier, read the annual report. This will give you insights into the culture and the terminology used to describe individuals within the organization. Again, you'll need this type of information as you prepare for your interview.

Should you research an organization's competition?

I think any time you can provide pertinent information about the organization, it indicates you've done your homework. That's extremely positive, and shows the interviewer you're interested. After all, if the interviewer gets the impression you're not interested in the organization, he or she probably is not going to be interested in you. Who knows...you may even reveal data about competitors of which the interviewer was unaware. That would be a big plus in your favor!

Isn't this a lot of work to go through just to get to the interview?

It is, but remember that earlier we talked about candidates who presented themselves poorly versus those who are successful. The difference between the two is **preparation**. Again, it also helps the candidate determine if the company is right for him or her. And, it'll help with the decision, once the organization has extended an offer.

What's next in the "pre-interview stage?"

Know yourself. Be ready to sell yourself. Know your transferable skills, and supervisory or management style. How you approach the job, and those who work above you, below you, and beside you. Be prepared with brief anecdotes about your work that illustrate the qualities the organization values, and emphasize your key accomplishments. In short, know the **benefits** you can bring to the job, and the interviewer can recognize. For example, you may have been involved in a project that will help demonstrate your leadership abilities. Honestly assess your employment background, and develop explanations for any weak points. If you're applying for a manager's job - but your resumes does not show management experience - be prepared to answer such questions. Prepare in advance a list of tough questions you might encounter, and make certain you have sound answers. Some of the most difficult ones to answer include: What are your strengths? What are your weaknesses? What do you like least or most about your current job?

Should you take previous appraisals or performance reviews along with you?

These would really help. If you have a current review or appraisal, bring it along. Don't show it unless you're asked, but you certainly can refer to it for the positive statements it contains. Something else that will help is **rehearsing** your interview - going over those potential questions that might arise, and becoming familiar with sound answers. Have a friend or spouse conduct the interview with you, so you can answer questions out loud and become more comfortable with the content.

As a seasoned Human Resources professional, what do you consider the most important elements to consider?

For me, that involves focusing on the knowledge, skills, and abilities the candidate brings to the job. For this reason, my questions center on previous successes, failures, and accomplishments. This helps me determine if a candidate has accurately represented his or her experience on the resume or application. I also try to find out, on a personal level, what the applicant's interest is in the position, and what is motivating him or her to apply for it. I also tailor my questions to the position for which I'm recruiting. Typically, I review the candidate's resume for anything that is lacking in the experience portion. For example, as mentioned, if I'm hiring a manager and the resume does not reveal this kind of experience, then I won't conduct an interview.

What's the final step in preparing for an interview?

Before we go on that all-important first interview, we need to understand how to dress the part. Know what to wear, and look the part. It's nice to think that appearances don't matter, but they do. You **must** make a good first impression! Looking your best may not get you the job, but the alternative certainly will detract from your chances.

Can you provide a few "dos and don'ts?"

There are some traditional ones. For men, when they're choosing a suit, stick with Navy blue or grey. For a shirt, white, ironed, cotton blend. Stay away from the silk shirts. As for the tie, it can be fashionable...but not bold. Sorry, **bow ties** are out! For socks, dark and over-the-calf. Avoid trendy haircuts. Facial hair is fine, as long as it's groomed. Try to avoid the cologne.

And, for the women?

For women, a suit with a contrasting blouse works best. Stick with one- to two-inch heels - no spike heels - and subdued, natural make-up. Again, try to avoid perfume, and stay with small earrings. Wear natural hose, and avoid the dark ones.

What about the "casual" dress codes observed by companies today?

Even though most organizations have casual or dress-down days, the interview uniform for today is still a nice suit. Again, this is where culture comes in. When researching an organization, you'll turn up information on how employees dress in the work place. Follow their examples. **Make certain** you find out what the standard is for the company before the interview. In fact, that should be on your "Interview Checklist" to ensure you're showing up in the right outfit. If you're unsure, call the organization's HR department. A good **rule of thumb** is to wear something that's somewhat dressier than the employees wear to work. **Never** wear jeans and a T-shirt, and unless you're interviewing with a famous designer, leave the logo stuff at home! A jacket is always a safe bet for men or women, with slacks or a skirt.

Now then, what about the interview itself?

Obviously, this is the **most critical** stage. Make certain your contacts with prospective employers are positive, friendly, professional, emanate quality, and are targeted to the right individuals. If you anger a secretary while arranging your interview - or alienate the receptionist when you show up at the appointed time - your interview may be doomed before it even gets under way. Interviewers are interested in how well you relate and work with others, beginning the minute you walk into the outer office.

How about some suggestions?

Make sure you arrive for your interview about 10 to 15 minutes early, and dress like the interviewer is likely to dress. If you're not certain, **be conservative**. Be yourself, but pay particular attention to grooming and your demeanor. Which is another reason to get there a few minutes early. This will give you time to duck into the rest room and check yourself out one more time. Granted, many organizations today dress business casual. However, you should dress in appropriate business attire unless directed to do otherwise by the interviewer.

What tips can you provide about handling the interview process itself?

Again, arrive at least 10-15 minutes early. Gather your thoughts and compose yourself. This also will give you time to meet those important support people. Do some information gathering - there usually are newsletters and informational brochures in the waiting area - and observe the working environment. This will provide additional information for you to use during the interview. **Remember**, late arrival for a job interview is **never** excusable. For this reason, it's also a good idea to make a "practice run" the day before the interview to ensure you know the route and where to park.

How about while you're waiting for the interview?

Be conversational, not nervous or fidgety. Smile, and look confident. Again, it's a good time to keep your eyes and ears open for things that will help during the interview. What are employees saying and doing? Maybe notice something on the secretary's desk or wall and strike up a pleasant conversation. This is an excellent time to begin winning people over to your side.

Okay, what's next?

Come prepared. Bring **at least three** copies of your professionally prepared resume, a note pad, and your list of questions. Don't forget your references, but don't provide them unless asked.

Tips on that first meeting?

Offer a firm handshake. This is your first encounter with the interviewer. If he or she holds out a hand and receives a limp, damp grasp in return, it's not a good first impression. So be firm, but not bone-crushing.

During the interview?

Maintain eye contact. Concentrate on one of the interviewer's eyes - it's easier to focus than trying to handle both. Don't stare, that shows aggression. Again, relax, smile, listen attentively, and respond succinctly.

What else?

Stay relaxed and be yourself. Project confidence, enthusiasm, and a positive attitude. You've done your research and you're prepared, so there's no reason you should not be confident! Again...be yourself. The person across the desk wants a glimpse of the "real you."

And then?

Ask questions. One of the worst things you can do when asked by the interviewer, "Do you have any questions for me?" is to say, "No." Remember, the interview is a two-way conversation, and this is your chance to find out more about the company, the job, and the culture - which will help determine if this is the right place for you to work. Asking questions demonstrates the importance you place on your work and career, and your interest in what the interviewer has to say. The research you've done will form the basis for your questions. Focus on the job, company, products, services, and people. This is **not the time** to ask about benefits and salary, unless the interviewer raises these issues. **Questions** you might consider include: What qualities are you seeking for a person in this position? What is a typical day on the job like? What are the most difficult aspects of this position? What projects would I be involved in now, or within the first year? What is the next step?

Are there questions an applicant should not ask?

Stay away from questions that might give the interviewer the wrong impression. You don't want to raise any warning flags. For example, asking, "Would I really have to work overtime?" Also, avoid questions about compensation, vacation, and time off. You don't want to sound like you're only interested in pay and play.

Any other tips?

Yes, there are a few things to keep in mind. Don't smoke, chew gum, tobacco, or anything else. Make sure you sit comfortably and erect, and don't dominate the interview. Time does not equal quality! Communicate effectively, and avoid the using slang. Be sure to thank the interviewer - and any others who joined the interview situation - for his or her time. Ask for business cards so you can send "thank you" letters. And, above all, **smile!**

> **Any final thoughts.**

Yes, let me recap. As the applicant, your job is to convince the interviewer you're the right one to handle the position. You need to make the most of your allotted time, which usually is only 30 to 45 minutes. Every question offers an opportunity for you to present your abilities and accomplishments. If you research the organization and the job - and you believe in your skills and work ethic - it should be easy for you to clearly demonstrate why you are the best candidate for the position. Once again, the interviewer will be sizing you up from the organization's point of view, and he or she **must recognize** what benefits you'll be bringing on-board. This is another reason for you to complete a detailed checklist - like the one offered in "**Knock 3 Times**" - for each interview situation. Finally, make certain of two things: If you're interested in the job, let that be known. Tell the interviewer you're interested, and ask how soon a decision will be made. And, most important, **immediately send "thank you" letters** to everyone involved in the interview process - from the interviewer down to the secretary and receptionist!

John/Jane J. Jobhunter

200 Main Street
Anywhere, USA 66666

(555) 555-5555

(**SAMPLE 1:** **Letterhead stationery**. This is 24-pound **Neenah Classic Linen** paper in Monterey Sand color. The ink is **PMS 534** [Navy]. "Knock 3 Times" is printed on 70-pound **Exact Offset** in Grey, also in PMS 534 Navy ink.)

(**SAMPLE 2:** **Letterhead Second Sheet** also is 24-pound **Neenah Classic Linen** paper in Monterey Sand color.)

John/Jane J. Jobhunter

200 Main Street
Anywhere, USA 66666

(SAMPLE 3: Letterhead Stationery Envelope is 24-pound **Neenah Classic Linen** paper in Monterey Sand color, printed in **Navy PMS 534** ink.)

John/Jane J. Jobhunter 200 Main Street (555) 555-5555
Anywhere, USA 66666

September 7, 200X

Mr. Elmer E. Employer
District Sales Manager
XYZ Corporation
300 First Street
Anywhere, USA 66666

Subject: Helping You Exceed Your Sales Goals

Dear Mr. Employer:

XYZ Corporation is well known as a leader in its field, and I would like to be considered for a position in its Sales Department. Currently, I am Sales Supervisor for the ABC Company, and am contemplating a career change. While I've enjoyed a successful association with ABC, my abilities have outpaced present challenges and opportunities available at the company.

I can make significant contributions to your organization in the areas of sales, business development, or marketing. For more than two years, I've been responsible for ABC's participation in conventions and trade shows, as well as overseeing telemarketing and sales promotion programs. Additionally, I supervise a staff of eight salespersons, and annually prepare and manage a budget exceeding $2.5 million.

A few of my sales and marketing accomplishments include:

- Generating more than 1,500 bona fide leads and inquiries from companies interested in ABC's products - resulting in more than **$5 million in new business**.

- **Reducing costs** of sales calls by providing qualified prospects, realistic business capture approaches, and effective introductory materials (all of which also **positively** impacted bottom-line performance).

(**SAMPLE 4: Introductory Letter** – Introduction and accomplishments letter seeking a Sales Manager's job. You should prepare this letter on a computer, and tailor it to the specific recipient at the organization to which you're writing.

Mr. Elmer E. Employer
September 7, 200X
Page 2

- **Training, instructing, and supervising** salespersons in the techniques of prospecting for business leads, making appointments, preparing and presenting proposals, and effectively closing sales.

- Planning, budgeting, implementing, and managing sales incentive programs prepared and implemented by outside motivation agency (most recent effort **generated more than $6 million** in additional sales).

In addition to spearheading business development and sales activities, I also develop and present intensive two-day work shops that train employees at all levels on preparing effective proposals. For creating and presenting these courses, I recently was commended by ABC's Chairman, awarded a $1,000 bonus, and credited with helping increase new business revenues by 25%.

If I may be of help as you consider my application - or should you have questions or desire additional information - please call me at (555) 555-5555. I look forward to talking with you soon.

Yours respectfully,

John/Jane J. Jobhunter
Sales Supervisor

John/Jane J. Jobhunter 200 Main Street   (555) 555-5555
Anywhere, USA 66666

September 14, 200X

Mr. Elmer E. Employer
District Sales Manager
XYZ Corporation
300 First Street
Anywhere, USA 66666

Subject: How John/Jane J. Jobhunter Will Benefit XYZ Corporation

Dear Mr. Employer:

Recently, I wrote you concerning possible sales or marketing job openings at XYZ Corporation for which my qualifications are suited. I since have updated my resume, and a copy is enclosed.

As mentioned in my earlier letter, I'm Sales Supervisor for ABC Company, and am contemplating a career change. I've enjoyed a successful association with ABC, but my abilities have outpaced the challenges and opportunities that currently are available with the firm. With this in mind, I'm seeking a Sales Manager position.

Confident you'll find a personal meeting interesting and mutually profitable, I'll call in a week to arrange an interview at your convenience. In the meantime - should you have questions or wish additional information - please call me at (555) 555-5555.

I look forward to meeting with you.

Yours respectfully,

John/Jane J. Jobhunter
Sales Supervisor

(**SAMPLE 5:** **Resume Cover Letter**. This second mailing introduces your impressive resume. Again, you should prepare this letter on a computer and tailor it to specific individuals at the organizations to which you write.

John/Jane J. Jobhunter   200 Main Street   (555) 555-5555
Anywhere, USA 66666

John/Jane J. Jobhunter
Sales Manager
"A Lucrative Addition to Your Winning Team"

Effectively combines EXPERIENCE **and** EDUCATION with strong sales skills and ability to exceed corporate and client expectations. Versatile, precise communication skills; conveys information effectively to all levels of staff, management and customers. Consistently sets new performance standards; provides excellent coaching and training to subordinates and peers. Uncompromising personal and professional ethics.

EXPERIENCE:
Sales & Account Management Military Logistics

DEMONSTRATED CAPABILITIES IN:

EDUCATION:
BS - Marketing - 1995
Anywhere University - Anywhere, US

KEY AREAS OF STUDY INCLUDE:

- Team Building & Training
- Psychology of Sales

- Customer Retention & Satisfaction
- Customer Service

- Cold Call Strategies
- Competition

- Oral & Written Communication
- Globalization

- Cost Reduction Procedures
- Econometrics

- Computer Operations
- Micro Economics

- Resource Analysis & Optimization
- Advanced Game Theory

(**SAMPLE 6:**   Resume – Printed on 24-pound **Neenah Classic Linen** in Monterey Sand color using Navy blue ink [**PMS 534**].)

EMPLOYMENT HISTORY:

ABC CORPORATION   Anywhere, US   4/1998 - Present
[Nation's leading ($1.5 billion) automotive widget production and distribution firm.]

Sales Supervisor, 2/2000 - Present
Sought-out for promotion by General Sales Manager. Ensure strong customer ties to obtain ongoing repeat orders and referrals. Train and supervise 8-person sales staff. Conduct monthly team-building and motivational work-shops. Coordinate scheduling and assign personnel to international conventions and trade shows.

Contributions:
- **Tripled inquiries and leads** from trade shows and conventions in one year, acquiring $9 million new business.
- **Increased referrals 25%** by maintaining excellent company relationship with existing customers and media.
- **Reduced staff turnaround 15%** / increased sales 30% through sales training, motivation and team building.
- **Skyrocketed relationship sales 150%** by ensuring existing customers received outstanding service.

Account Representative, 4/1998 - 2/2000
Traveled to automotive manufacturers throughout the U.S. to initiate business relationships and resolve customer issues. Convincingly presented marketing materials, tailoring each presentation to individual customer needs.

Contributions:
- Awarded "**Rookie Salesman of the Year**" by outselling remainder of 10-person sales force with personal new customer sales exceeding $1 million in 1999.
- **Requested to conduct sales training** by Sales Supervisor, causing sales team to exceed quarterly goals by 13% and 15% last 2 quarters of 1999. (Previous 3-year high was 11% above goal.)

DEF COMPANY   Anywhere, US   10/1995 - 4/1998
[Tri-state military radar component manufacturer with annual sales exceeding $900 million.]

Account Manager, 7/1996 - 3/1998
Maintained sales, customer inventory and satisfaction of four major aircraft developers in assigned territory.

Contributions:
- **Boosted component sales 25%** through tracking customer inventory of competitors' components and determining most opportune time for sales calls.
- **Improved customer retention** by providing a personal level of service beyond position requirements.
- **Regularly exceeded quarterly goals** via strong product knowledge and excellent presentation skills.

Sales Trainee, 12/1995 - 7/1996
Learned all aspects of Account Manager duties. Accompanied various salespeople on customer calls.

Contributions:
- **Assisted in development and delivery of presentations** for old and new component lines.
- **Personally developed highly successful presentation** used comprehensively throughout tri-state area.

SMITH'S AUTO SALES   Anywhere, US   6/1993 - 9/1995
[Largest car dealership in the state with annual earnings upwards of $15 million.]

Leasing Manager, (1/1994 - 9/1995)
Leased Sales Trainee, (6/1993 - 1/1994)
Sold vehicles and leases, ensuring all paperwork and support activities were kept 100% up-to-date. Worked evenings and weekends while full-time student.

Contributions:
- **Promoted to management** position after only 6 months with company.
- **Developed and implemented** highly successful large corporation fleet sales method, selling over 2,000 cars during first month of program.
- Conceptualized and developed lease tracking system to automate direct mail lease renewal campaign.

U.S. ARMY   Georgia, Oklahoma and Saudi Arabia   5/1989 - 5/1997
[4 years active duty followed by 4 years U.S. Army Reserve.]

Logistics & Field Training

John/Jane J. Jobhunter 200 Main Street (555) 555-5555
Anywhere, USA 66666

Good morning, Mr. Employer.

My name is John/Jane J. Jobhunter. Recently, I wrote you inquiring if a sales or marketing job was available with your company for which I'm qualified. Did you receive my letters and resume?

(wait for answer.)

Good!

I'm calling this morning to see if we could meet, and I could tell you more about how my qualifications and experience could benefit XYZ Corporation.

Would 9 a.m. on Tuesday, September 25, be convenient?

Fine, Mr. Employer. I look forward to seeing you then.

In the meanwhile, thank you…and have a nice day.

(**SAMPLE 7: Telephone Script**. Tailor this for your call on September 18 [third week]. Memorize and rehearse. . . don't just read over the telephone!)

John/Jane J. Jobhunter 　　　　　　　　200 Main Street　　　　　(555) 555-5555
　　　　　　　　　　　　　　　　　　　　　Anywhere, USA 66666

Interview Checklist (12 steps to help you succeed):

This Checklist will help you remember pertinent items so you can respond with "on-target" answers. It also will remind you to complete essential "follow-up" activities. Don't read from the Checklist - but keep it handy to review toward the conclusion of your interview. This will ensure you don't overlook benefits you bring to the job, or questions you need to ask: For example, "I'm interested in the job you've described, and wondered how quickly you intend to fill the position?"

For help with interview questions, refer to our "**Effective Interview Techniques**" CDs at http://stores.lulu.com/propman01. Provide information for the following items before **and** after your interview:

1. Day, date, and place of interview:

2. Data about Interviewer (collect via telephone):
   A. Name
   B. Title
   C. Company
   D. City, State, and Zip Code (nine-digit)
   E. E-mail address
   F. Telephone number
   G. Cell phone or pager number
   H. Facsimile number

3. Your major Accomplishments (list and prioritize):
   A.
   B.
   C.
   D.
   E.

4. Types of work you've performed (managerial, supervisory, skilled):
   A.
   B.
   C.
   D.
   E.

(**SAMPLE 8:** **Interview Checklist**: Complete one for each interview to ensure you don't overlook a benefit or key point to make during the session. By preparing the Checklists, you'll firm in your mind the answers to typical interview questions, as well as those you want to ask the interviewer. It also will help you remember certain activities - such as the **all-important** "Thank You" letter!)

Interview Checklist (12 steps to help you succeed), continued:

5. Pertinent facts about yourself (mainly, key accomplishments):
   A.
   B.
   C.
   D.
   E.

6. Your responses to tough questions (answer these):
   A. Why are you leaving your current job?
   B. What are your strengths?
   C. What are your weaknesses?
   D. Would you be willing to relocate?
   E. What are your salary requirements?

7. Your questions for the interviewer (make certain you have):
   A.
   B.
   C.
   D.
   E.

8. Benefits you bring to the organization (use Item 5. for starters):
   A.
   B.
   C.
   D.
   E.

9. Others involved in interview process (secretary, associate, or boss):
   A.
   B.
   C.
   D.
   E.

10. Lessons learned from interview (what went right and wrong):
    A.
    B.
    C.
    D.
    E.

11. Persons to whom "Thank You" letters must be sent (see Item 9.):
    A.
    B.
    C.
    D.
    E.

12. Clothing worn to interview (so don't wear same to follow-up interviews):

John/Jane J. Jobhunter   200 Main Street   (555) 555-5555
Anywhere, USA 66666

References

Samuel S. Smith, Owner
Smith's Auto Sales
3333 West 14th Street
Anywhere, USA 63636

George G. George
National Sales Manager
DEF Corporation
1212 East Long Drive
Anywhere, USA 62626

Alvin A. Allison
General Sales Manager
DEF Corporation
1212 East Long Drive
Anywhere, USA 62626

Robert R. Roberts, Jr.
Executive Vice President
Everywhere Aircraft Company
Everywhere, USA 10909

Professor Charles C. Charles
Dean, School of Business
Anywhere State University
First and Second Streets
Anywhere, USA 64646

Major Raymond R. Raymond
Commanding Officer
3rd Infantry Regiment
Anywhere Army Reserve Center
Anywhere, USA 65656

(**SAMPLE 9:** **Reference Sheet**. Printed on 24-pound **Neenah Classic Linen** paper in Monterey Sand color, in **Navy PMS 534** ink. **Make certain** you have talked with your references to ensure their telephone numbers and addresses are current, and also as a courtesy to let them know they may be contacted.)

John/Jane J. Jobhunter 200 Main Street (555) 555-5555
Anywhere, USA 66666

Question: Why are you leaving your present employer?

Answer: Primarily, I'm seeking more challenges and opportunities than are available with ABC Corporation. While I've enjoyed working for ABC, I'm capable of assuming new responsibilities that currently don't exist within the company.

Question: What sort of salary are you expecting?

Answer: Salary is only one of the criteria I'm considering in changing careers. The most important, of course, is the job itself. Another is the people for whom and with whom I'll be working. I have a general salary range in mind. What figure has been established for this position? (If pressed, give a range: mid-20s, low-30s, or upper teens, for example.)

Question: What is your biggest strength?

Answer: (Here are a few good responses to this one.)
- ► I'm a firm believer in setting priorities, and meeting deadlines, objectives, and budgets.
- ► I'm extremely effective at managing and developing people.
- ► I can obtain results through others, and by delegating assignments.
- ► I recognize and utilize good talent, and offer constructive criticism as needed.
- ► I can effectively motivate employees.

Question: What is your biggest weakness?

Answer: Often, I expect others to work at my pace. Sometimes, I take on too much myself.

Question: What interests you most about our company?

Answer: Compatibility! From the research and reading materials I've complied on XYZ Corporation, it appears most in line with my career goals and aspirations.

(**SAMPLE 10:   Interview Questions and Answers**. For examples of **the top 20 questions** that employers ask - as well as excellent responses to use during interviews - order our "**Effective Interview Techniques**" CDs at http://stores.lulu.com/propman01
Also includes insights into what the job interviewers seek and expect during these meetings.)

John/Jane J. Jobhunter   200 Main Street   (555) 555-5555
                                   Anywhere, USA 66666

September 26, 200X

Mr. Elmer E. Employer
District Sales Manager
XYZ Corporation
300 First Street
Anywhere, USA 66666

Subject: Thank you for the interview!

Dear Mr. Employer:

I enjoyed meeting and talking with you, and discussing the job opening in your district. The Sales Manager's job sounds exciting and challenging, and it perfectly matches my qualifications and background. As you'll recall, I have extensive in-depth experience in introducing sales systems and developing sales opportunities; as well as training and motivating people who work for me.

When our meeting ended, you expressed concern over XYZ's recent expansion into Internet sales activities, and creation of a Web Site. I did not have an opportunity to tell you, but I developed and implemented a similar web site for ABC Corporation. Over the first three months, our sales jumped by 25 percent! For this reason, I feel qualified to help you introduce, operate, and manage this new sales activity.

Again, thank you for the opportunity to interview, and for the additional insight into XYZ's operations. I look forward to hearing from you in the near future. Until then, best regards.

Yours respectfully,

John/Jane J. Jobhunter
Sales Supervisor

(**SAMPLE 11: Thank You Letter**. This letter is a **must**, and represents yet another opportunity for you to strengthen a point you made, or bring up a benefit you may have overlooked. This document also is printed on 24-pound **Neenah Classic Linen** paper in Monterey Sand color, using **Navy PMS 534** ink.)

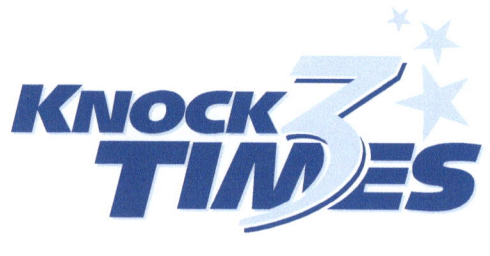

(a division of McCormick Associates, LLC)
32 Jefferson Road
St. Louis, Missouri 63119-2935
(314) 961-7335

(**SAMPLE 12: Note Paper**. Here are a few sheets on which you may take notes as you read "**Knock 3 Times**. . .". Or, to use as you research, prepare for interviews, or for "Lessons Learned" following your successful interviews.)

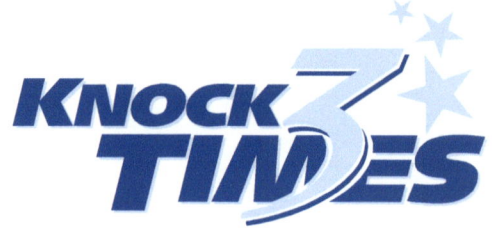

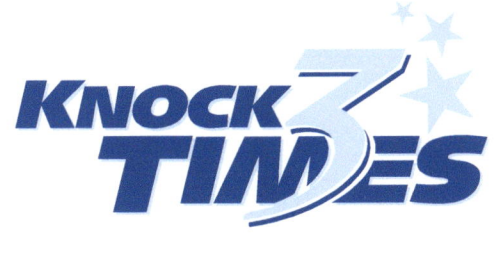

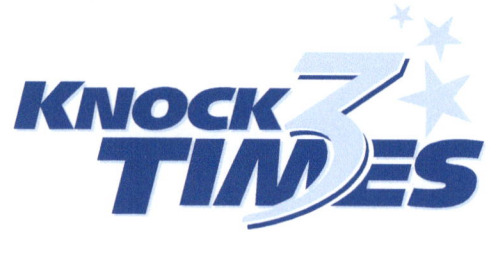

www.ingramcontent.com/pod-product-compliance
Lightning Source LLC
Chambersburg PA
CBHW041519220426
43667CB00002B/43